D1486878

How to Build Log-End Houses

Drake Publishers Inc. New York · London

How to Build
Log-End Houses

by Robert L. Roy

Photography by Dan Jerry

Drawings by Marie Cyburt Taluba

Lovingly dedicated to Jaki,
who did more than her fair share
in transforming Log End Cottage
from the stuff of dreams
to reality

SEP 7   1979

Published in 1977 by
Drake Publishers, Inc.
801 Second Avenue
New York, N.Y. 10017

Library of Congress Cataloging in Publication Data

Roy, Robert L.
    How to build log-end houses

    1. Log-end houses. I. Title.
TH4818.W6R69   694   77-72392
ISBN 0-8473-1608-4
ISBN 0-8473-1551-7 pbk.

Design-Harold Franklin
Art Direction-Amy Horowitz

Printed in the United States of America

Illustrations appearing on pages 14 and 15 from page 67 of
An Age of Barns by Eric Sloane. Copyright©1967 by Funk &
Wagnalls Publishing Company, Inc. Reprinted by permission
of Thomas Y. Crowell Company, Inc.

Illustration appearing on page 25 from page 169 of In Harmony
with Nature by Christian Bruyére, and Robert Inwood.
Copyright©1975 by Christian Bruyére. Reprinted by permission
of Drake Publishers, Inc.

CONTENTS

PREFACE

My wife, Jaki, and I have chosen a homesteading lifestyle: we are "back-to-the-landers," if you like. We believe that to get through times of high inflation and unemployment, as well as to maintain a 98.6° body temperature in a world of rapidly decreasing fossil fuels, it is necessary to be as independent of "the system" and its money-based economy as possible. So we make electricity with a windplant instead of plugging into the national grid; we heat and cook with wood (which grows faster on our homestead than we can burn it as fuel; we grow a significant part of our food, and hope to improve at this; we patch rips in our clothes instead of buying new ones; and we have bypassed huge annual expenditures on rent or mortgage by building our own cottage, largely with recycled materials – and "stovewood masonry." Thus we have secured Food, Fuel, Clothing, and Shelter–the "necessaries of life," as outlined by Thoreau–at relatively low cost.

While it is true that building out of log-ends suits our adopted lifestyle, both economically and aesthetically, we do not believe that this style of building is in any way limited to homesteaders; rather, it is well-suited to that larger group called owner-builders, of which homesteaders are only a part. Log-end houses are an alternative to log houses and can be in harmony with any wooded area. Our cottage is a chalet type of our own design, but log-ends could be delightfully incorporated into many different architectural styles, including ranch, A-frame, barn-style, or any of the various log cabin designs. The only qualification is that the framework of the house be both rigid and seasoned, whatever building style is chosen. In this book, I have included a chapter dealing with this subject in more depth.

Other readers may find that they wish to use log-ends in a part of their house only, in combination, say, with stone, logs, or even modern two-by-four framing. I hope *Log End Houses* will help these people to incorporate stovewood masonry as an interesting design feature in their building. Log-ends might make an unusual room divider between living and dining areas, for example. The possibilities are limited only by practicality and imagination. This book's purpose is to advise you of the former and to stimulate the latter.

R.R.

Log End, 1977

TRACKING
THE ELUSIVE LOG-END

Books about building, especially those with an owner-built slant, get plenty of shelf space in bookstores nowadays. One can find literature on building houses out of hides, paper, plastic, sod, and rammed earth. Build-yer-own-log-cabin manuals are plentiful. But information is sparse concerning stovewood (or *log-end*) masonry, that type of building where very short logs are laid up in a wall like a rank of firewood. My wife, Jaki, and I first encountered the method some years ago in a book showing various styles of building in the nineteenth century. I have not been able to find another edition of that book, but I remember that the reference was brief, one or two pictures with little practical information. A few months later, while on a land-hunting tour of the States, we took a week's employment in Arkansas helping to build a traditional log cabin of heavy pine logs. We discovered that even working together we could not easily lift the logs, much less maneuver them into position. We aren't giants.

In Scotland we lived in a stone cottage with walls twenty inches thick. Stone is appealing, but we wanted to avoid building a house within a house, which is necessary to supply adequate insulation in Upstate New York, where we finally bought some abandoned farm land. We hadn't forgotten the log-end idea, and when we saw a color photograph of the inside of just such a cabin in a magazine, we were sold. Log-ends it would be!

But how?

Having labored for a mason in Scotland, I knew that the bond between mortar and wood is weak. We used to cast lintels in wooden forms and the forms always came loose from the concrete easily. Jaki and I questioned the strength of a log-end structure.

It seemed that the safest method of building with log-ends would be within a strong post-and-beam framework, so that the mortared log-ends would not themselves be load-supporting. And if we used big enough timbers, we thought, we could approximate the pleasing appearance of the Elizabethan "black and white" houses on the exterior and have the warm atmosphere of an English country pub inside. Later, we read in Eric Sloane's *An Age of Barns* (Ballantine, 1974) that German settlers in Wisconsin built barns and other structures with stovewood masonry within a post-and-beam framework.

The only other reference to log-ends that we were able to find was in Ken Kern's *The Owner-Built Home* (Charles Scribner's Sons, 1975). We learned that settlers in Canada's Ottawa Valley built stovewood walls. A man who runs a sawmill near our land said, yes, he'd seen such houses up near Cornwall, Ontario. *Hmm;* we thought, *not too far...*

The seventy-five-year-old gentleman from whom we'd bought our land—and who'd built over ninety houses in New York's North Country—offered to drive us up to Canada to see if we could find examples of stovewood masonry. "I'm not too old to learn new tricks," said Tom. And sure enough, after stopping to chat with a few people in the district, we began to find a few log-end buildings. First, we came across a

"Stovewood Masonry"

"Barn near Crandon, Wisconsin.

an Indiana Grain Barn

WOOD BLOCK

Spring House in Montana

1-1. Stovewood masonry. (From *An Age of Barns*, by Eric Sloane, courtesy of T. Y. Crowell)

large dairy barn built in 1956. The owner was
happy to show us the structure, but, as he hadn't
built it, he could give us few details about its
construction. What surprised us was that—except
for two-by-six framing around doors—the log-ends,
ten inches long, were load-supporting. And it did-
n't look like the barn was in any danger of col-
lapsing. Incidentally, the farmer's house was
also built of log-ends, but they'd been plastered
over and we could learn little of the construction.

A little later we came across an old log-
end schoolhouse which had been converted to
a horse barn. The owner told us the building was
100 years old. We could see that most of the
log-end work was still in good condition, although
one panel within the post-and-beam framework
was crumbling away, probably aided by the
horse. The log-ends were eleven inches long
and were held together with a lime mortar. If
memory serves me, the builders had mixed
horsehair in with their mortar, probably to re-
tard cracking. (We had seen horsehair plaster
in our cottage in Scotland.) Needless to say,
we were delighted to find a log-end structure
a hundred years old. *Encouraging...*

It was late afternoon and it seemed we wouldn't find any more examples easily, so we started home. To our amazement, we came upon a man laying up the walls of a log-end barn within a post-and-beam framework. We stopped, of course. The builder told us he had built quite a few log-end structures, including an A-frame for a customer in central Ontario. The gable ends were stovewood masonry. Although he never returned to the A-frame after the job was finished, the builder did come across the owner five or six years later and asked him how the place was holding up. Grand, said the owner, no problems to report.

We asked the builder if he could offer us any advice.

"Not much to it, really," he said. "Use dry wood, wet mortar, and throw an extra shovel of lime in with your mix."

Simple stuff, but words of infinite wisdom to two would-be owner-builders starving for information. We returned to our temporary shelter, a 12' by 16' shed, intoxicated with the idea that, yes, it could be done and, if done right, a log-end structure could last a century under the most severe conditions.

The most important part of stovewood
masonry is the condition of the log-ends.
They must be *dry*, not almost dry. They
should be cedar. The builder in Canada
was using sixty-year-old cedar fence posts
and rails, cut to eight inch lengths. I can't
think of a better source of material if you're
in a hurry to get started. Even so, I would
recommend sun- or stove-drying the cedar
fence log-ends for at least a month before
laying them up, just to be sure.

    Cutting and drying log-ends is your first
job, even before starting the foundation.
Stack them outside like firewood, with air
space between ranks and a waterproof cover
on top. Or stove-dry them inside with plenty
of air circulation in the drying area.

    While old posts and rails are a good source
of dry material, and can make an attractive
wall, they have certain drawbacks, not the

least of which is their decreasing availability. Folks in the suburbs pay fancy prices nowadays to enclose their yards with the old fences. Other drawbacks to the split rails are that a lot of the material will be rotten, knarled, or awkwardly shaped (as a result of twisting). Also, the predominantly triangular cross-sectional shape of a rail fence is not as conducive to fitting into a wall pattern as round logs of varying diameters.

In the November/December 1976 issue of *Harrowsmith*, a magazine for Canadian back-to-the-landers, there is a short article about a "cord wood" workshop built by a young Canadian in 1973. Most of the builder's "log butts," as they are called in the article, are cut from replaced telephone poles and wooden guardrail posts that he obtained from utility companies and the highway department at very low cost: two dollars apiece for the old poles, nothing for the guardrail posts. But even better than the price was the fact that the old posts and poles are as aged as they'll ever be and will not shrink or check. Pictures accompanying the article show that the resulting walls can be attractive, though there appear to be dark stains around the log-end edges, probably because the poles had been impregnated with creosote.

Another advantage of the salvaged pole idea is that it enables a prospective owner-builder to consider a log-end home even in a nearly treeless area such as the Plains States.

Still, if you have your own cedar trees, price, convenience, and—in my opinion—aesthetics, point toward using them. Or perhaps striking a bargain with someone nearby who has a cedar stand. If cedar does not grow nearby, use pine, Douglas fir, or western larch. With any wood other than cedar, use a preservative on the exterior. Our log-ends are 100 per cent cedar and we have an average of three feet of overhang all around our cottage, so we feel confident in letting the log-ends age naturally.

An advantage of stovewood masonry is that you can use trees which, because of their size, would be unsuitable for any other type of building. You will need a lot of small and medium-sized pieces in the one-to five-inch diameter range. This means that practically all of the tree can be utilized. Remember that you can use fallen trees, and, in fact, these have the advantage of being partially dry. Some cedar stands have a high proportion of trees with a hollow core, which can extend four feet or more up the trunk. Don't be discouraged. Log-ends cut from these trees can be very attractive features in your wall. And they seem to dry more evenly, without checking. Small-diameter core holes can be plugged with a wad of fiberglass insulation and mortar. Clean out larger holes with a chisel and put a small log-end or "bottle-end" inside. (Bottle-ends are discussed in Chapter 5.)

You can use trees which appear to be badly bowed, because a log-end is such a small segment of the tree that the bow will hardly appear. But avoid bushy trees, as there will be too many branches to trim. The spot on a log-end where a branch has been trimmed will usually be irregular, making that piece difficult to fit in. You will have to

use a certain amount of these log-ends unless you have a lot of wood to waste, but
it is a great time saver to use fairly clear
trees if possible. Also, trimming a nine-inch
log-end of stubs with a saw or axe is awk-
ward and a little dangerous. Better to trim
as close to the tree as possible before felling
or immediately after.

At any time of the year it is good to bark
the tree soon after felling it, and the same
day if possible. The easiest time of the year
to bark any softwood is spring, when the
rising sap loosens the tight bond between
bark and wood. In April, you can practically
pull the bark off with your fingers alone.
Sabre, our German Shepherd, had a grand
time yanking eight-foot strips away from
the log. The trouble with spring felling is that
the trees are much heavier with water and
take a lot longer to dry properly. The driest
standing wood will be found in late fall,
when the sap has run back into the ground
to protect the tree against freezing. The
trouble with autumn felling is that the bark

is reluctant to let go of the log.

As stated, we barked in the spring, so the job was easy enough to do with an axe, a trowel, and a German Shepherd. All you have to do is force the blade of the axe or trowel in below the bark at a tangent to the log. Then work the blade right and left. If freshly cut, the cedar bark will pull away from the wood like a banana peel. Later in the summer, Jaki and I helped friends bark cedar logs which had been cut a few weeks. It was a completely different job. Armed with peeling spuds made from truck springs (a big improvement over a trowel and an axe) we were still lucky to complete one fourteen-foot log in an hour. The moral: Peel fresh.

Though peeling logs was not a problem for us, it can be a troublesome task, especially on dry logs or logs which are not barked soon after felling. Christian Bruyére's *In Harmony with Nature* (Drake, 1975) includes an illustration by Robert Inwood showing clearly one method of making a handy peeling spud.

Making a Peeling Spud Out of an Old Shovel

2-1. Peeling spud. (From In Harmony with Nature, by Christian Bruy-ère and Robert Inwood, courtesy of Drake Publishers)

Though I have not tried this tool my-self, it makes a lot more sense than the short-handled spuds we used on our friends' logs. The long handle should give the user a vastly superior leverage. Tom Hodges, in a short article in *The Mother Earth News* (July, 1976), has another idea. He says, "My debarker-I've also heard it called a 'peeling spud'- is simply a garden hoe with the blade straightened out. To make one yourself just take an old hoe, heat its 'neck' until the metal is malleable, and bend the blade back until it forms a 165° angle with the tool's handle. Sharpen the business end of the device and presto! You've got a tool that's guaranteed to make easy work of any bark-stripping job. To use the spud, just anchor or wedge your post so it won't move, stand over it, and dig in. With a little practice, you'll soon be able to peel off two- to three-foot strips with one swipe."

When to cut and how long to age the log-ends are matters dictated largely by individual circumstances. The ideal situation would be to fell and peel in the fall and store the wood – perhaps in six-foot lengths – somewhere dry and warm for the winter. In the spring, move the logs to the building site, cut them into ends, and air-dry them until you're ready to lay up walls.

Our own method was somewhat more work, but the results were worth it. We moved to the land in the spring, built our shed, and began gathering cedar. We were able to secure 40 per cent of what we needed from our own cedar grove. We could have taken more, but we did not want to deplete the grove. The rest of the cedar came from a variety of sources: leftover pieces from two friends who were building log cabins, a pick-up truck load a farmer gave us, and three similar loads for which we paid five dollars a load. We made the mistake of stacking our cedar in the shade, hoping to dry it slowly in order to minimize checking. Next time, I will dry the wood as fast and as much as I can and the heck with the checks.

Late that summer, when our post-and-beam framework was up and the roof finished, we cut the cedar into nine-inch log-ends and stacked them in the framework for the winter. We covered the exterior of the framework with half-inch insulation board and spent several days stuffing the gaps between the log-ends with wads of fiberglass insulation. In December, when the front door and all the windows were finished and the two stoves installed, we moved into the cottage, glad (and a little sad) to be out of the shed.

The woodstoves dried the log-ends for a good six months before the weather and the garden allowed us to get back to work. Considerable checking had appeared in the end-grain. (See Figure 2-2.) Beginning in June, we

2-2. The log-ends were stacked to dry through a winter. I am pointing out a check that formed during the drying process. The panel on the left is still covered with a half-inch insulation board that helped to protect us from that first North Country winter. The log-end panel on the right is complete.

dismantled and rebuilt (with mortar) each panel, one at a time. By "panel" I mean a section between posts, roughly 5' by 6'6" in most cases.

The drying method described above involves a lot of handling of materials. If, like us, you're trying to live in the house at the same time, tempers can run short as living conditions become more and more chaotic. But it works.

Other questions to ask before building are "What length should the log-ends be?" and "How many will I need?" The two questions are closely related, in that the composite answer determines how much cedar you need to cut.

The length of log-end—the width of your wall—should be determined by how much insulation you require. In general, softwoods have an "R" value of 1.25 per inch, but my feeling is that cedar, because of its unusual porosity, must have a greater "R" value than that, perhaps as great as 1.5. The higher the "R" value of a material, the greater its resistance against heat loss. Here are comparative "R" values for a few other building materials

Material	R Value	R/Inch
8" concrete block	1.00	0.13
12½" of stone masonry	1.00	0.08
4" common brick	0.80	0.20
1" hardwood board	0.91	0.91
6" fiberglass blanket insulation	19.00	3.16

Three and one half inches of fiberglass, or R11, is the *minimum* recommendation for the walls of framed houses in a cold climate. We used 9" log-ends, which might give us something in excess of an R12 insulative factor, but weighed against this figure is the fact that conductivity is considerably greater parallel to the grain than against it. We would have used 10" log-ends, except that they would have been too proud of our barn beam posts, which are predominantly 8" by 8". Using nine-inchers, then, was a value judgment based mostly on aesthetics. You may decide on a more functional approach; longer log-ends. As it turned out, our cottage is small enough and our roof insulation thick enough that we have no difficulty heating with our woodstoves.

In a warmer climate, or for a summer cabin, I think 6" log-ends would be sufficient, but in that case you may be able to use a solid mortar rather than the insulating method we describe in Chapter 4.

How many log-ends? Perhaps our experience will help answer this question. Figure 2-3 is a schematic drawing of the completed panel shown in Figure 2-4. It is a typical panel, with the same variety of sizes used throughout the cottage. We do have a few 10" and 11" log-ends, but probably fewer than twenty in the whole structure. The diameters are the actual sizes taken from the panel itself, rounded to the nearest inch. Odd-shaped pieces are converted to the diameter of a circle of the same area. The panel has 8.56 square feet of stovewood masonry and fifty log-ends, roughly 5.8 log-ends per square foot. Broken down statistically:

Diameter of log-ends 1" 2" 3" 4" 5" 6" 7" 8" 9"
Number of log-ends 4 11 11 5 4 7 4 3 1

      Unless you cut much bigger trees than ours, this breakdown can be considered fairly typical, as we laid up all our panels carefully, avoiding large areas of mortar. Simply figure the square feet of masonry required and multiply by 5.8 to get the number of log-ends you need. Add at least 15 per cent to this

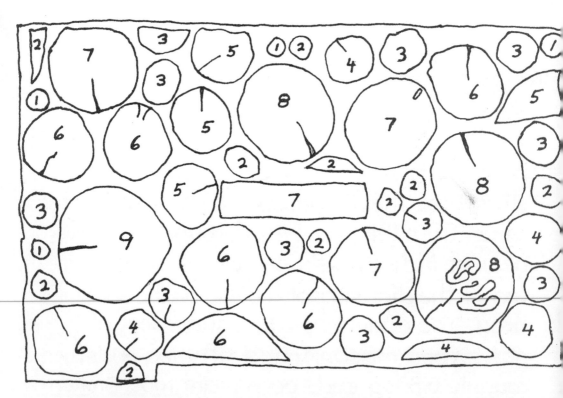

2-3. A diagram showing the diameters of the log-ends pictured in Figure 2-4.

2-4. This panel, the obverse of the one being laid up in Figure 4-8, is held together with sawdust mortar.

figure to allow for error, rejects, and a better selection. (Leftover log-ends make grand kindling.) Do not worry about distribution of sizes. If you use all of the good log-ends you can get from a tree, the distribution of size should take care of itself.

While on the subject of log-end size, here's a hint about cutting your trees into lengths for removal from the forest. Decide on the width of your wall before heading for the woods! Cut your logs, especially the first two or three you take from a tree, to a length that is a multiple of your log-end size. This saves a lot of waste as well as one saw cut. For example: six-footers (72") will accommodate 6", 8", 9", or 12" log-ends without waste - and they are easy to carry. Five-foot-ten (70") will make 7" or 10" log-ends. When you actually cut the logs into ends, you will lose ¼" with each cut. Our "nine-inch" log-ends, for example, really average 8¾". And don't be too fussy about their all being identical lengths. You'll need to work fast or it'll take forever to cut 3000 ends. Let 'em vary a bit. A half-inch either way is fine. Gives your wall a more interesting relief.

Log-ends can be cut with a chain saw, but the finished product is not as neat as with a circular saw. And cutting a 16" piece in half with a chain saw is risky. We rented a portable circular saw with its own gasoline engine. It has a spring-return table upon which the log is placed. The table—with the log—is turned into the blade. Fast. Easy. Safe. Many farmers have similar set-ups which they run off their tractors with belts.

Friends helped us the two days we cut log-ends, and we were able to establish a very efficient system. One person fed me the wood, I cut it, another delivered the ends by wheel-barrow, and someone else stacked them in the framework for winter drying.

THE FRAMEWORK

First, a word about the foundation. We have
a full concrete block cellar. We feel that it
is imperative that the foundation not be able
to move, or even vibrate, under a wall of
stovewood masonry. For this reason, I cannot recommend a pillar-type foundation,
unless the span between pillars is short
and the plates (or beams) are extra heavy
duty. Better to go with a poured concrete
foundation, concrete blocks, or stone.

The framework of the house is as important to log-end building as the stovewood
masonry itself. Despite our seeing in Canada
the 1956-built barn which used log-ends for
the support structure, I tend to shy away
from relying on stovewood masonry as a load-
supporting medium. A good post-and-beam
framework should do *all* the load supporting.
You should be able to fill in the walls of such
a structure with baled paper, chicken wire,
plaster... almost any darn thing. But log-
ends are nice.

There are good books available on post-and-beam construction and I suggest you borrow or buy one. I will say something of our own post-and-beam system, however, as it has worked well for us. All of our posts and beams are old hand-hewn barn timbers— every man jack of 'em a slightly different dimension! In fact, the size varies from one end of a beam to the other. Generally, though, the beams are in the 8" by 8" to 10" by 10" range. Obviously, a lot of extra measuring and notching was necessary. Tedious? Yes, but worth it, as it's good to be square and level when the time comes for putting up the roof rafters. And old barn beams *are* beautiful, if you're lucky enough to find them at a reasonable price.

But the greatest advantage to using old barn beams is that they are bone-dry, the single most important consideration in stove-wood masonry. Yes, you could have dimensional beams cut from your own trees, and these would save the days of measuring and fancy cutting of hand-hewn beams, *and* they would almost certainly be cheaper, unless you can score a bargain on old beams, *but* they will shrink away from your stovewood masonry, even if you air-dry them for two years. Swiss master-builders of the last century air-dried even five-by-eights for three full years before using them, and they were not building out of log-ends.[1]

If you *are* willing to plan years in advance and have spruce or hemlock on your property, haul 'em to the nearest sawmill and have 'em cut to exactly the same cross-sectional dimension. When you finally do build with these beams, the dimensional cutting will save you lots of exacting work. Beams 4½" by 9" (full sizes given) would be a good size for a nine-inch wall, but bear in mind that the beams will be 27 per cent heavier per linear foot than 4" by 8" members. Also, four-by-eights can be cut from a much smaller tree and will dry a bit faster. Your decision depends on

1. Drew and Louise Langsner, *Handmade*. (New York, Harmony Books, 1973), p. 132.

what's available and how wide the wall is to be. The framework establishes the width of the wall if the beams are to be exposed both inside and out. If you *are* able to plan three or more years in advance, get your log-ends cut and stacked, too. You'll thank yourself for it later.

Another possibility is kiln-drying, if there is a wood-drying kiln near you, but kiln-drying of material thicker than three inches would take an awful lot of time in the kiln and add expense to an already expensive process. Still, there's nothing wrong with framing with three-bys. It's good sturdy stock and you could double or triple them up at the corners if you wanted.

Many large sawmills have their own kilns. I don't have a lot of experience with kiln-dried wood, though I used to buy it when I was in the water-ski-making trade, but I would be cautious with regard to any great claims made by the sawmill people. People's ideas of "dry wood" vary greatly *and you want it as dry as you can possibly get it.* I have bought so-called "kiln-dried" two-by-fours that will squirt you in the eye when you drive a nail into 'em. Old Tom, our builder friend, says that kiln-drying is inferior to drying wood naturally in properly stacked piles outside. The Swiss master-builders agree with him. They believed that kiln-drying crisps wood to death.[2]

But I'm not trying to put down kiln-drying. If done properly, and if the wood is left in the kiln long enough, the process may be the only viable way for you to make an early start on a post-and-beam framework of dry timbers. I *do* advise caution, however, and the same attention to detail that should be a part of every step of building with log-ends. If you're not sure of the dryness of your wood, try the following test, which I have seen conducted successfully by an owner-builder friend of mine. At least a foot from either end, cut a short section of the beam in question—three inches is plenty. Take an accurate measurement of the width (cross-section) of the piece to within a sixteenth of an

2. *Ibid.*, p. 133.

inch. On a four-by-eight beam, for example, you are mainly concerned with shrinkage on the four-inch dimension. Bake the sample in a 300° oven for six to eight hours. (Remember that wood can burn at from 400° to 600°.) Take another accurate measurement. If the shrink-age is less than ⅙", your wood is dry enough. If greater than ⅙", the post or beam could shrink away from your masonry. An aid in bonding your masonry to the framework is to nail lots of old nails to the side of the posts which will be adjacent to the log-end walls. Drive them to within ¼" of home to keep them from getting in your way and don't forget to leave a clearway for insulation if you decide to use the insulating method descibed in the next section. The nails will give the mortar something to grab.

But back to the framework...

Our largest span between posts is eight feet, measured on center. This situation occurs at both gable ends, so we chose our largest and best pieces as corner and gable sup-port posts. Along the side walls, no span is greater than six feet on center. Many experienced builders say our cottage is "over-built," but this term puzzles us. Is a house over-built because it lasts three hundred years instead of one lifespan? Anyway, our intentions were to put a sod roof on in the future and we wanted to be sure that the framework would be able to support the tremendous weight involved.

Figure 3-1 shows a layout of the cottage, and Figures 3-2, 3-3, 3-4, and 3-5 show four views of the framework. After these photographs were taken, we added diagonals along the sidewalls just as we did at the gable ends. The diagonals are paired three-by-tens with a three-inch insulated space between. (The photographs show only a single three-by-ten diagonal.) Diagonals add rigidity to a post-and-beam structure by the formation of triangles. In modern framing, plywood serves the same purpose. It seems to me that the chances of stovewood masonry working loose of the framework are greatly diminished in a rigid structure.

As a point of interest, our floor joists and roof rafters are also old three-by-tens, two

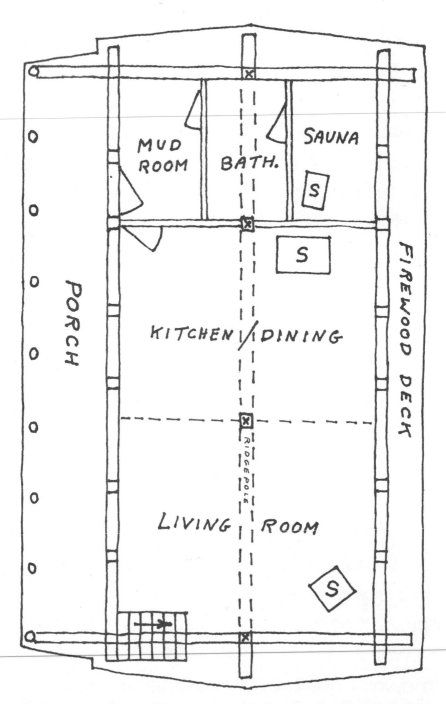

MUD ROOM

BATH.

SAUNA

S

S

PORCH

KITCHEN / DINING

FIREWOOD DECK

RIDGEPOLE

LIVING ROOM

S

3-1. A plan of the main floor showing the location of posts and beams. The ridgepole spans four tall posts, marked X. Sleeping lofts are above the living areas and small rooms; the kitchen-dining area has a cathedral ceiling. There is a full basement with a room and a root cellar. The locations of stoves are marked S.

3-2. Post-and-beam framework, north gable end.

3-3. Post-and-beam framework, south gable end.

feet on center. We were lucky to find two
excellent buys on three-by-tens from different
people who were demolishing an old school
and an old hotel not far from our homestead.

Our diagonals are in every second panel.
Alternate panels frame our windows and the
front door. All hinges, then, are fixed to heavy
timbers, and all windows have a barn-beam

3-4. The posts of the west wall. Later a porch was added, using the cantilevered three-by-tens for supports.

3-5. Post-and-beam framework. The interior beams at the far end support the sleeping loft.

3-6. A Swiss post-and-beam house infilled with masonry. We had completed our cottage before we saw this house, and were surprised
and pleased to find the same pattern of diagonals in alternate panels that we used in both our side walls. (Compare Figure 3-3.) The
house shown is probably close to two hundred years old. (After
a photograph from Handmade, by Drew and Louise Langser,
courtesy of Harmony Books, Crown Publishers).

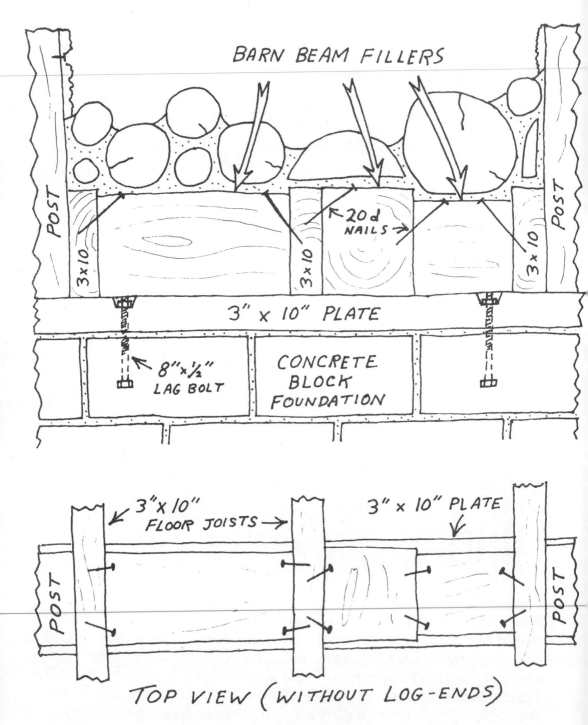

BARN BEAM FILLERS

POST

POST

3×10

3×10

←20d NAILS→

3×10

3" × 10" PLATE

8"×½" LAG BOLT

CONCRETE BLOCK FOUNDATION

3"× 10" FLOOR JOISTS →

3" × 10" PLATE

POST

POST

TOP VIEW (WITHOUT LOG-ENDS)

3-7

3-7. In our cottage we used three-by-ten floor joists, twenty-four inches on center. The joists cantilever out over the foundation plates (also three-by-tens), supporting the front porch and the back firewood deck. We found it convenient to fill in the space between joists with segments of barn beams left over from the framework. The barn beam fillers add support to the joists and establish a fairly flat surface upon which to be laying log-ends. The barn beam sections are hidden from direct view by the decking and inside flooring, except in the basement.

 The three-by-ten plate is bolted to the foundation by 8"x ½" lag bolts which are well cemented into the last course of concrete blocks. We used three bolts for each ten-foot section of the plate, leaving the threaded end three inches above the top of the block foundation.

3-8 (Below) Find out where to drill for the bolt holes by laying the plate upon the bolts and whacking the plank stiffly with a hammer. Then remove the plate and drill the half-inch holes where the bolts have left depressions in the wood.

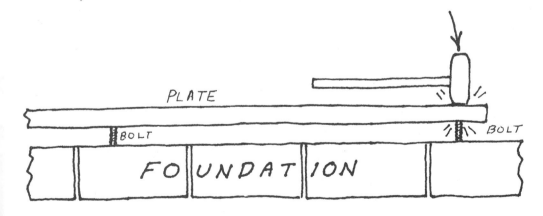

PLATE

BOLT   BOLT

FOUNDATION

3-8

3-9.(Below) It will be necessary to chisel enough wood out of the top of the plate to receive the washer, nut, and socket attachment.

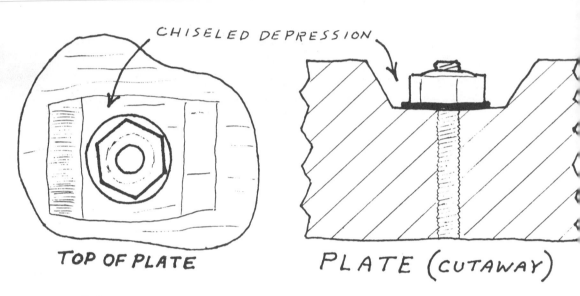

CHISELED DEPRESSION

TOP OF PLATE

PLATE (CUTAWAY)

3-9

If you haven't got a socket set, leave the bolts 3½"
above the foundation and use a crescent wrench to tighten the
plates down. Then chisel a little out of the bottom of the barn
beam fillers so that they fit over the nut and flush on the plate.
    Use eight-inch-wide by quarter-inch-thick strips of fiberglass insu
lation between the foundation and the plate, between the plate and th
barn beam fillers, and between the fillers and the floor joists. Tightenin
the bolts will then provide a draft-free seal above the concrete blocks.
Judicious use of twenty-penny nails will do the same job for the fillers
(Hint: Creosote the plates a few days before using them!)

sill. These precautions also were taken to ensure that the mortar would not work loose from the framework.

A final note: Heavy framing, as I have described, is just as physically demanding as building a traditional log cabin, so we measured and cut each section on the ground and then reassembled it in place with the help of friends. But there are only nine beams in our cottage that required help, compared with sixty or more long logs for a cabin of comparable size.

BUILDING
WITH LOG-ENDS

Your framework is finished. It is dry. You are ready to lay log-ends. As this subject is the meat of the book, I will go into some detail and not assume previous masonry experience on the part of the reader.

Tools. For mixing mortar, you will need a good wheelbarrow, a hoe, a shovel, and a bucket for carrying water. For cleaning the wheelbarrow—a must as soon as it is empty—the same bucket and some sort of stiff scrub brush will suffice. It is good to have a different bucket for carrying mortar. You need a mortar board. I use a two-foot-square piece of plywood, but a wooden mortar board must be kept damp, especially on hot days, or it will drain the mortar of its moisture. For laying log-ends by the insulated mortar method described below, a small trowel is useful. I use an old pointing trowel I bought at an auction in Scotland. A regular mason's trowel with, say, an eight-inch blade is also handy, especially where wider bedding is necessary. Make a pointing tool by bending the tip of an old kitchen knife slightly.

To prepare log-ends for the wall, you will want some sort of rasping tool to smooth the hairy edges of the end grain. These fibers get in the way of pointing and can prevent a good bond. We've found that a Dragon Skin rasping block is the perfect tool for the job. A circular sanding motion will save on Dragon Skin, but get a couple of extra sheets anyway. You'll use 'em. (See Figure 4-1.)

Your log-ends, especially those over four inches in diameter, should have fairly substantial checks in them from drying. I'm wary of log-ends that don't. The middle three or four inches of these checks should be stuffed with fiberglass insulation. Different sizes of screwdrivers are useful for stuffing checks. (See Figure 4-2.)

A chain saw, hand saw, axe, splitting wedge, and hammer are all useful to eliminate pesky protrusions and to split a log-

4-1. Preparing the log-ends with Dragon Skin.

4-2. Stuffing the checks with fiberglass.

end to fit in a particular space.

A word of caution: Use rubber mason's gloves or your hands will be cracked and your fingers full of nasty "cement holes" by the end of the second day.

The Mix. You've got a day's worth of log-ends prepared and you're ready to mix. Ah, the mix! The magic formula that's going to hold your masonry together. This was the part of the whole operation that scared us most. We spent a winter speculating on various mixes. In Scotland, I had talked with the mason I used to work for, but I think he was more than a little skeptical about building out of log-ends in the first place. Did we want a mix that would "give" with the expansion and contraction of the log-ends, or did we want a hard, stiff mix? In *An Age of Barns*, Eric Sloane mentions "lime mortar" and the Canadian builder we'd met said, "Throw an extra shovel of lime in with your mix." Okay, lime mortar does not have the strength of Portland cement, but neither does it have the hardness.

Clearly, we would have to experiment. We chose as our experimental panel the smallest in the cottage, a two-foot square below a front window. Our mix was 10 shovels sand, 1 shovel white Portland cement, 2 shovels masonry cement, and 1 shovel lime. Masonry cement contains Portland and lime, so I think it's fair to say that this recipe is equivalent to a 2½ or 3 to 1 mix using just masonry cement. We laid up the panel and waited two or three days for it to harden. By then the mortar was hard but not completely seasoned, since it takes over a week for mortar to season. We decided to lay up two more panels using the same mix. Then a couple of days went by and we re-examined the small experimental panel. Tiny cracks were developing in the jointing, not many, but cause for concern, we thought. Also, we weren't completely happy with the color. Our idea in using white Portland – and the lightest sand we could find – was to have a very light colored background for the log-ends so that the completed panel would contrast with the dark barn beams, which were creosoted outside and walnut-stained inside. Our experimental panel was bluish-grey. So, to make a less rigid mix and to lighten the color, we altered the recipe slightly to 12 sand, 1 white Portland, 1½ masonry, and 2 lime. This mix, I believe, is roughly equivalent to a 3 or 3½ to 1 sand to masonry ratio, except that the extra lime gives an airy quality to the wet mortar and decreases the final hardness. This is the formula we stuck with for the rest of the cottage, except for one more experimental panel.

We knew that Cornell University had been doing some work with sawdust mortar, and we had plenty of cedar sawdust in a heap where we had cut our log-ends the year before. So, we replaced half the sand in the previous formula with an equal number of *heaping* shovels of clean sawdust. (Note: Always use consistently sized shovels when following any formula.) Converting heaped shovels to normal size, the formula is 6 sand, 9 sawdust, 1 Portland, 1½ masonry, 2 lime.

Now, as I write, many months have passed and I am able to compare the final results. Here is a breakdown:

Mix	Characteristics
A. 1 OS, 1 P, 2M, 1 L	Bluish-gray. Very hard. More and slightly wider joint cracks than Mix B
B. 12 S, 1 P, 1½ M, 2L	Very light gray. Not quite as hard as Mix A. A few hairline cracks.
C. 6 S, 9 sawdust, 1 P, 1½ M, 2L	Greenish-gray. Rough finish, but hardly any cracks at all. Hardness like Mix B.

The sawdust mix seems to "work" with the log-ends better than the other mixes, and it seasons more slowly because it retains the moisture longer, but it is more difficult to point and leaves a rough surface because saw-dust keeps sticking to the pointing knife. In addition, it would seem that the sawdust mix has to be better insulation. Mix A, in my opinion, is too strong, and greater mortar shrinkage is the result.

If you have—or can get—the sawdust,

and don't mind the rough surface (it looks good, but seems to collect dust faster), I must say that Mix C is the best of the three we tried. But Mix B is also fine.

There are two minor nonstructural problems with all of the mixes we used—cost and complexity. White Portland is about three times as expensive as the regular gray. And it's somewhat of a hassle—and even confusing first thing in the morning—to be dealing with three different bags of binding material. After we finished our masonry, we met with a friend who had been rebuilding an old stone tavern nearby. Using regular gray Portland, lime, and sand only—no masonry cement at all—he was getting a much whiter mix than we, cheaper, and with less confusion and inconvenience. If I were to start over on another log-end house, I would try a simpler mix to eliminate the dark-colored masonry cement altogether. Based on my experience as a mason's laborer in Scotland, my own experiments outlined above, and observations of my friend's mix on his tavern restoration, I feel that a mix of 10 sand, 2 ordinary Portland, and 2 lime will give a very light color and have the qualities required for stovewood masonry. It's an easy formula to re-member and has the advantage of being divis-ible by two; that is, a larger mix could be made by the addition of 5 sand, one Portland, and one lime. Eight shovels of sawdust could be substituted for four of the sand, making 6 sand, 8 sawdust, 2 Portland, and 2 lime. Remember that I have arrived at this formula by interpolation and *have not tested it*, so try a panel, let it age a week, and decide upon its virtues for yourself. (Which you should do with *any* mix.) Like every mason I have ever met, you will probably settle on your own favorite recipe anyway, and—like everyone else's—it will be the best.[1]

    Keep in mind that all of the mixes discussed

---

1. *May, 1977.* The log ends have experienced a second winter's stove dry-ing, this time *in situ*. It has now been a year since we laid up our first panel. A few small log-ends are slightly loose in their surroundings, making us glad that we have a good sturdy framework to our cot-tage. The sawdust panel is still perfectly tight and is clearly superior to the others. I will employ sawdust mortar with all stovewood ma-sonry in the future. It's well worth the extra effort. If you can't get enough sawdust from cutting your log-ends, you can usually get all you want from a sawmill. Use the heavy sawdust that a chainsaw or a ripsaw makes, not the fine stuff found where finished work is done, like a cabinet maker's workshop.

in this section are meant for use in a structure where a strong framework is supporting the load. The *Harrowsmith* article mentioned in Chapter 2 tells of a workshop with 12"-inch thick log-end walls that are themselves load-supporting— like the barn we had seen in Canada. The builder's ratio was three masonry cement to five sand with one shovel of Portland thrown in with each mixer load, a much stronger mix. He used a power mixer because of the tremendous amount of mortar used, as is evidenced by the photographs accompanying the article. I would estimate that in a given area of wall he used twice the mortar we used. The article states that the builder relies for strength on the *mortar, not* the log-ends. For structural reasons, I do not endorse stovewood masonry as a means of supporting a load in a house, but it would be misleading to state that it cannot be done.

Mixing. Log-end work takes time. Mortar seems to go a long way, and you want it to stay fresh. A powered mixer, then, is really no advantage. Hand mixing is kinder to the environment, it is cheaper, and the mortar is easier to fine-tune for wetness. Dry-mix the ingredients in a barrow. Work 'em over good with the shovel. Then gradually mix in the water. Pretty soon the consistency will be more conducive to mixing with a hoe than a shovel. Mix thoroughly. Scrape the bottom of the barrow for that dry sand and lime. (See Figures 4-3 and 4-4.)

4-3. Dry-mix the mortar thoroughly with a shovel.

The mortar should be wet, but thick enough so that the bedding will support the log-ends without spilling all over the ground. It should hold its shape when placed halfway up on an adjacent log-end. If it won't, it's too thin-or you need a little more practice with the trowel.

Insulation. Cedar is excellent insulation, but solid mortar is next to worthless,

4-4. Whip it with a hoe. Scrape the barrow for dry material lurking in the corners.

so we devised a method of insulating the joints themselves. Our first job each day was to brush the posts and beams to remove dust. Then we tacked a two- to three-inch-wide strip of fiberglass insulation—⅜" thick is plenty—along the center of the bottom plate and up the posts. (See Figure 4-5.) These

4-5. First steps: Tack strips of insulation along the beams. Lay a double bed of mortar.

strips were cut from batts or rolls of insulation with a skill knife. As we used nine-inch
log-ends, this left room for a three-inch bead
of mortar on each side of the insulation. I don't
think there would be room for the insulation
strip on walls of less than eight-inch thick-
ness, but I wouldn't go thinner than eight
inches anyway, except perhaps six inches on
a summer cottage or in southerly climes. In
those cases, use a solid bed of sawdust mortar and forget the fiberglass.

  As you lay up the wall, continue to snake
the strip of fiberglass over and under the log-ends.
(See Figure 4-6.) Where three log-ends meet,
stuff in a wad of insulation to fill the gap.
Tacking the strip along the posts keeps it
from constantly falling into your work. We
tried tacking a strip to the top beam, but it
sometimes got in the way of the last course,
making it hard to get a tight fit without push-
ing out the insulation. We learned that it was
easier to jam the insulation in at the top after
all the log-ends were in place.

  This method of insulating the mortar
is our own discovery and has worked well

4-6. (Top, left) (a) Weave strips of fiberglass over and under the log-ends. Here a "cradle" has been shaped for a medium-large log-end.

4-6. (Above) (b) The cradle is filled with an eight-inch diameter end.

4-6. (Left) (c) After bedding and a strip of insulation are placed, the next piece – in this case a bottle-end – is laid.

for us. Yes, it slows progress down quite a bit, but isn't a warm house worth an extra week on the job?

Laying Up. The first course is very important. Try to get away from the flat plate and into a random pattern as quickly as possible. If you lay a first course of log-ends of the same diameter, you'll get stuck into a pattern which is hard to break... and, paradoxically, hard to keep up! Aesthetically, masonry looks good if it is totally random and if it is very carefully done to a pattern. It looks bad if it looks like someone tried to incorporate a pattern, and failed. And it looks bad if an intended random wall becomes patterned.

We like the random look; mistakes are less obvious, the wall is strong, and it incorporates all different diameters–and shapes– of log-ends. The latter feature helps ensure that you deplete the various sizes of log-ends in your pile at an equal rate, leaving a good selection right to the end. One of the little tricks of stone masonry which applies equally well with log-ends is to keep a variety of pieces handy. Probability dictates that the right log-end is almost certain to be in a pile of, say, fifty random pieces, but sometimes, especially when you get close to the top or into a corner, it will be necessary to split a specific piece from a clear-grained log-end.

Good pieces to start with are log-ends split in half, or, for corners, split in quarters. Another handy shape is what we call a "slat-end." A slat is the first piece taken off a log when it is being squared for lumber. We scored a couple of pick-up truck loads of slats at no cost when a friend was having his cedar milled.

And remember: most log-ends have at least one fairly flat side!

The diagrams in Figure 4-7 show the importance of the first course. Once you establish a random line, you will no longer have true "courses." Rather, you will be dealing with individual spaces of varying sizes. The wall will almost build itself by telling you what the next piece should be. This is as it should be for a truly random wall. Also, it helps keep the joints small. (A quarter inch to one inch is good. Any smaller makes for difficult pointing. Any greater and it's hard to insulate, looks funny, and wastes mortar.)

When I suggest that the wall will build itself, I don't mean to say, "Stop concentrating." Sometimes chance will get you into an unwanted pattern. The first warning is when you start using five or six log-ends of the same size in the same location. Log-ends of the same size fit beautifully into a hexagonal pattern, like a honeycomb, but you will deplete one size very rapidly if you fall into this lazy man's trap. On the other hand, you may want to feature just such a configuration in the midst of a random background. This type of planned deviation can be extremely effective, and is discussed in the next section.

Another good reason to stay alert is that

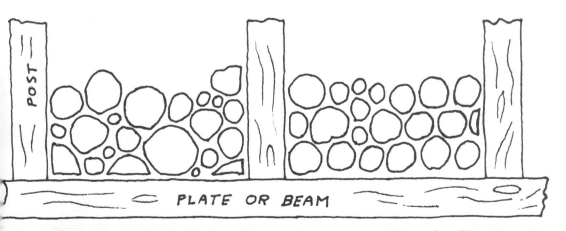

4-7. The first course establishes the random pattern. (See also Figure 2-3.)

chance will rarely provide good opportunities to lay your 9" to 12" log-ends. Big log-ends require a "cradle," and you will have to provide for this requirement once in a while. This shouldn't slow you down, though, because one 10" diameter log-end gets a lot of wall up in a hurry. (See Figure 4-8.)

Other points to remember during the laying up:

1. Lean over your work once in a while and eyeball it up and down, right and left. Is the work plumb? On large panels, check with a level now and again.

2. Stand back from the wall once in a while. Is the work balanced? Does it please the eye? Why? Why not?

3. Avoid putting one joint right over another. This basic rule of building is even more important with log-ends because there is little bond between wood and mortar.

4. The going gets tough near the top. If possible, get someone on the other side of the wall to stuff insulation, lay bedding, tell you if a piece is too long or too short, and place log-ends. Sometimes, in close quarters, a log-end will only

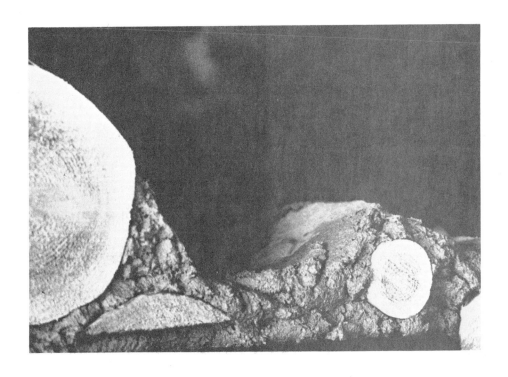

4-8.(a) Cradling...(b)...for a big one.

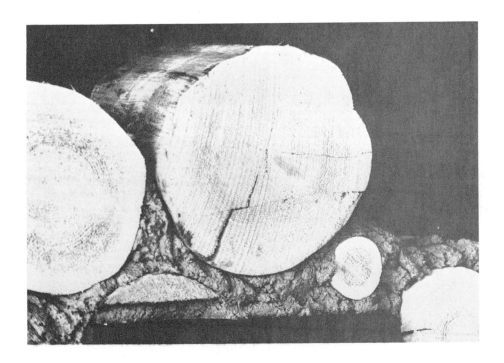

4-8.(c)Pointing...(d)...the experimental panel.

fit in from the other side! A good way to fill the final joint is to push the mortar off the back of your trowel and into place with your pointing knife.

    5. Slat-ends and half-logs are handy on the last course and along side framing, but avoid over-using them.

    6. Don't be afraid to use odd-shaped pieces. They'll add interest to the wall.

    Pointing. This is one of the most important parts of the whole job. Many people think that pointing is purely decorative, to smooth rough cement. Not so. Proper pointing greatly *strengthens* the wall by tightening the joints and reducing the chance for mortar cracks. The pressure of the mortar against the wood under the pointing knife gives the best chance for a good bond. So put a fairly stiff pressure on the knife as you draw it along between the log-ends, but not so much to push it into the insulation cavity.

    But, yes, pointing *is* decorative and is important to the finished appearance. There are many kinds of pointing and tools to point with, but we feel that the cedar, and not the

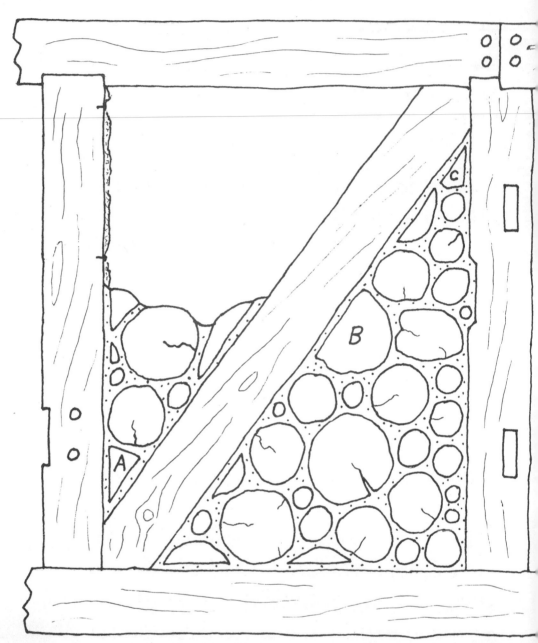

4-9. Diagonal supports add strength and beauty to post-and-beam construction, but they don't make stovewood masonry any easier. Filling
the triangle on the lower right is especially difficult. Apply the same tech-
niques as when filling in close to the top of a panel. Splitting special
pieces will be necessary more often than usual, and the work will go mo
slowly. By comparison, the upper-left-hand triangle in this panel is eas
once the first three or four log-ends are fitted. In this panel, ends A, B,
and C were cut specially to fit.

mortar, is the predominant feature of stovewood masonry, so we accent the wood with
a simple recessed pointing, the log-ends ¼"
to ¾" proud of the mortar. Recessed pointing
helps provide the interesting relief of a log-end
wall. Another mark against fancy pointing, such
as raised V-joint, is that the joint is very small
where log-ends are tangent and wide in the space
between three log-ends, so a time-consuming
job becomes difficult and tedious.

Pointing should be done while the mortar
is still plastic. Be careful on hot days not to put it
off too long. Usually, there will be enough mortar
squeezing out of the joints to point with, but
save a little at the end of a day's laying in case
there are substantial holes to fill. If you've got a
really big hole to fill, stuff some insulation in
first. Pointing is illustrated in Figures 4-8c and d.

After Work. When you stop for the day,
wash your tools and cover your work, especially
the outside, with a wet towel. This is a great
aid in seasoning the mortar *slowly,* minimizing
shrinkage. Leave the towel on the work the next
day, too, especially if the panel gets the direct
sun. Another method which we used is to wet

the joints down with a brush for a day or two after each laying up. This was one of our first jobs each day.

I cannot overemphasize protecting your work against fast drying. An extra five minutes care at the beginning and end of each day may well mean the difference between a solid wall and a drafty stack of rubble.

LAYING UP LOG-ENDS: A STEP BY STEP GUIDE

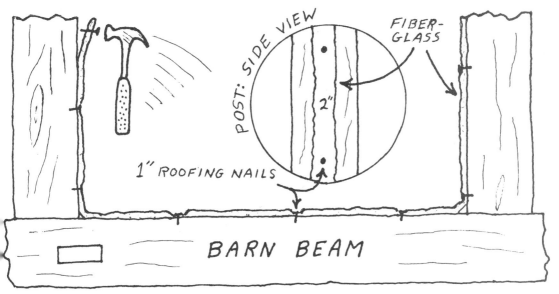

FIBER-GLASS

POST: SIDE VIEW

2"

1" ROOFING NAILS

BARN BEAM

4-10. (Above) Tack two-inch-wide strips of fiberglass insulation that is ⅜ inch to ½ inch thick along the plate beam and up the sides of the posts to prevent its falling into your work.

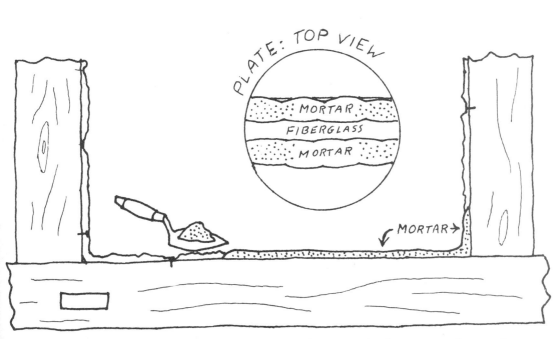

PLATE: TOP VIEW

MORTAR
FIBERGLASS
MORTAR

MORTAR→

4-11. (Below) Using a small trowel, lay a bead of mortar, ⅜ inch to ½ inch thick, along each side of the insulation on the plate beam and a few inches up the posts.

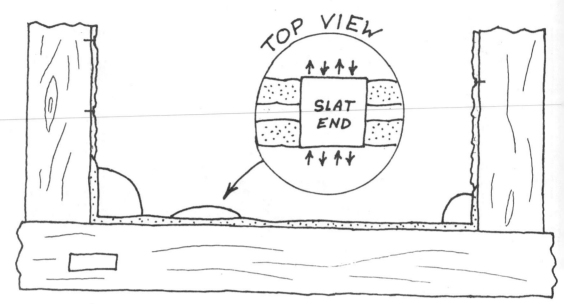

4-12.(Above) Good pieces to start with are quarter log-ends and slat-ends. Lay them firmly in place, applying enough pressure so that the mortar squeezes out a little. A slight sliding motion back and forth at right angles to the plate will assure a good tight bond.

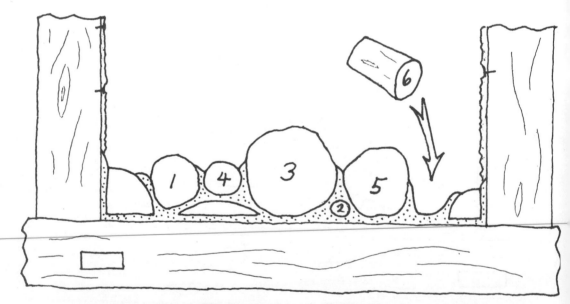

4-13.(Below) Complete the first course, bedding and insulating up the sides of adjacent log-ends as necessary. Numbers indicate suggested order of placement. (See also Figure 4-7.)

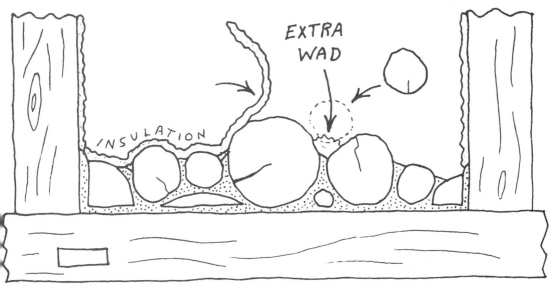

4-14. (Above) To save time and labor, lay long strips of insulation whenever possible. Pack an extra wad in wherever a triangular space will be formed by a log-end capping two other log-ends.

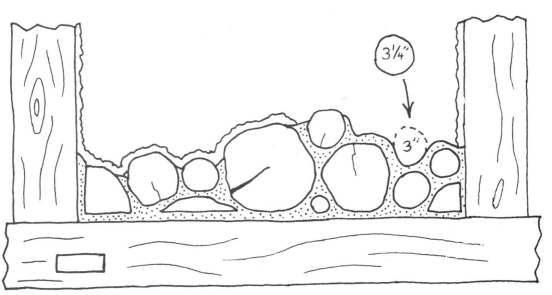

4-15. (Below) Try to form the shape of the next log-end with your bedding, but just a tiny bit smaller than the piece you have in mind, so that it'll force a little mortar out, assuring the best possible bond.

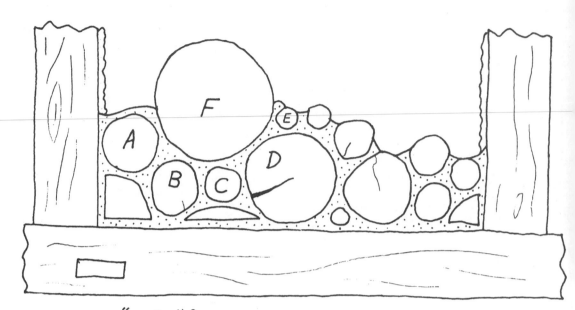

4-16. Plan "cradles" for your big log-ends, again, so that the cradle is just that wee bit smaller than the end you are going to lay up. Log-ends A, B, C, D, and E, with the mortar bed above them, form the cradle for the large end F. Use a little pressure and that slight sliding motion to squee the mortar out a little. Don't be too neat with your mortar. Make a b of a mess. A mess of mortar on the ground is a sign of a good bond. If you set the mortar board under your work and up against the plate, you should be able to salvage most of the mortar that falls off the wall. You can catch the stuff on the other side with your hand or th

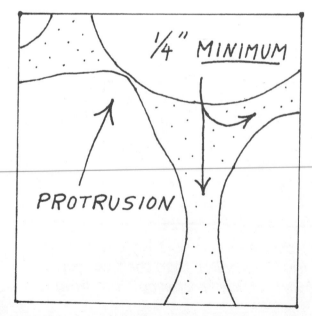

trowel. Wear gloves. Don't pres sure your log-ends so much tha the one you are laying up squish down and touches the one belov Leave at least a quarter inch o bed between ends where they a tangent; one half-inch is better. A protrusion on a log-end can o ten be fitted into the triangular space enclosed by three ends, b sometimes there is no way to a- void a protrusion touching an adjacent piece and establishing the gap between them.

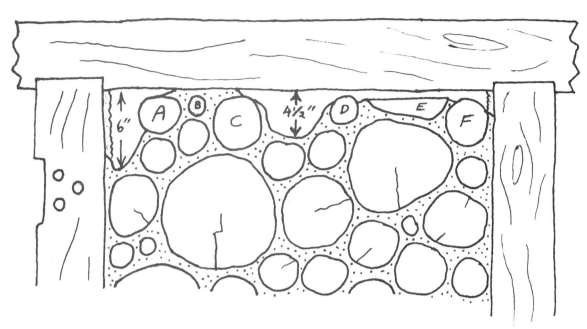

4-17. It gets tougher near the top. A, B, C, D, E, and F are easy to find if you have kept a good selection of small ends and slat-ends handy. The upper left-hand corner wants a slat-end, but to get a good fit, you split a couple of inches off one that is the right shape, but too big. The other space will be filled nicely with half a medium log-end. After bedding, take a measurement before you split, allowing one-half inch for the topmost mortar joint.

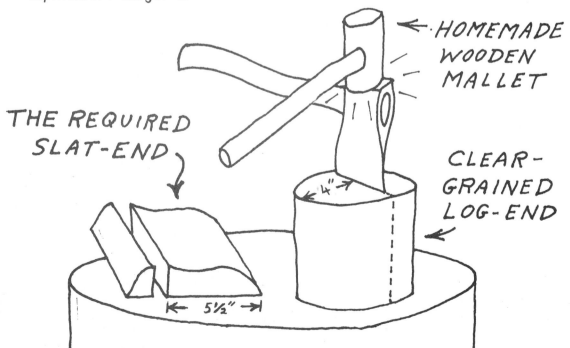

THE REQUIRED SLAT-END

HOMEMADE WOODEN MALLET

CLEAR-GRAINED LOG-END

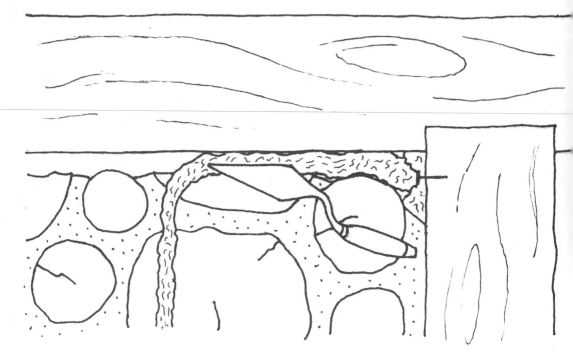

4-18.(Above) Use the point of your trowel to stuff insulation over the las course.

4-19.(Below) To fill the final gap, push mortar off the back of the trowel with the pointing knife.

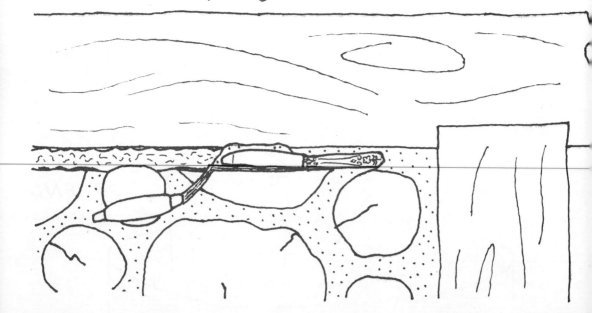

4-20. The finished panel. The "beam-end" in the middle breaks the monotony of the round shapes. Pointing tidies up the panel and helps strengthen the mortar joints. When the house is finished, and the mortar is well seasoned, you can clean dirty log-ends and beams of any dusty mortar with a whisk broom. Particles of mortar do not adhere well to wood.

SPECIAL EFFECTS

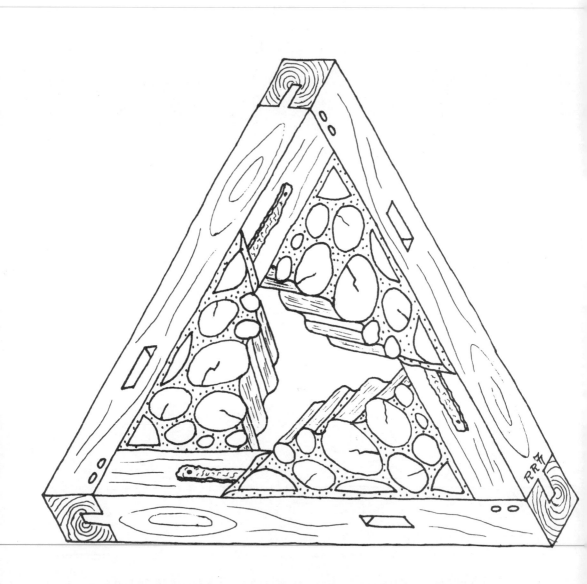

5

There are many good reasons to build
with log-ends: wood unsuitable for other styles
of building can be used; the work is not as
physically demanding as for a traditional log
cabin; and the consistent width of dry cedar
is an excellent insulation in cold climates. (In con-
junction with a cellar, a log-end house stays
cool in the summer, too.)

Still, the first appeal of log-ends is almost
always visual. Somehow, stovewood masonry
is faintly reminiscent of the gingerbread cottages
in storybooks. Together with a sturdy post-and-
beam framework, the look is similar to that of
the English "black and white" houses, and yet,
at the same time, a certain Scandinavian flavor
is present. The log-ends have such a natural
beauty of their own that it would almost take
a conscious effort to lay up a wall which was
not pleasing to the eye. The different colored
patterns of the end grain and the random checks

that form during drying *almost* guarantee success. Almost.

But if you take your time, pay attention to detail, improvise, and, above all, use your imagination, your wall will be personal, unique, and very beautiful. I will discuss a few ideas in this section which I hope will illustrate that stove-wood masonry can be a highly creative medium.

Relief. Recessed pointing by itself should ensure a three-dimensional look to your wall, but further interest is added by deliberately recessing a log-end or allowing one to protrude, especially if the log-end has some special color, texture, or natural design. Or wood-burn a log-end with a hot wire and feature it in relief. A good example of relief is shown in Figure 5-1.

Variety of Style. As mentioned earlier, we were able to secure a couple of loads of scraps left over from cedar logs used for traditional log cabins. They ranged in length from one to three feet and were all uniformly milled to six inches. For variety, and to use this valuable windfall, we built three panels with the log-ends laid up horizontally, in courses. The result is shown in Figure 5-2. By a coincidence, the roof

5-1. A good example of relief.

slope of one of the cabins was the same as that of our diagonals, and we only had to cut three or four pieces to fit. Some of the pieces were very wide, 12" to 14". These we laid together in a course to make a boot shelf for our mudroom.

 Pattern: We stayed with the random style throughout the house, except for a few creosoted "beam-ends" which we placed in

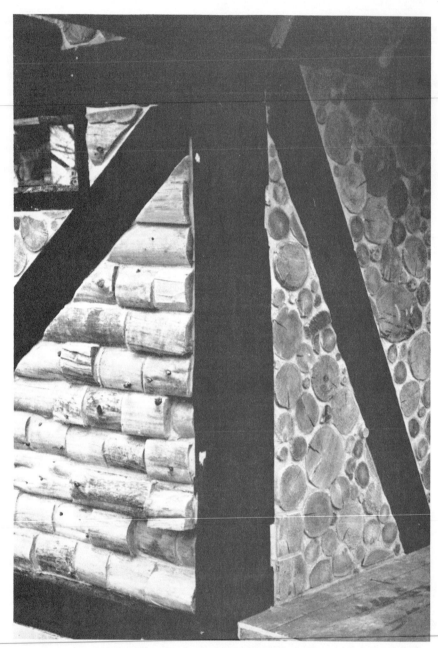

5-2. Two different styles of stovewood masonry.

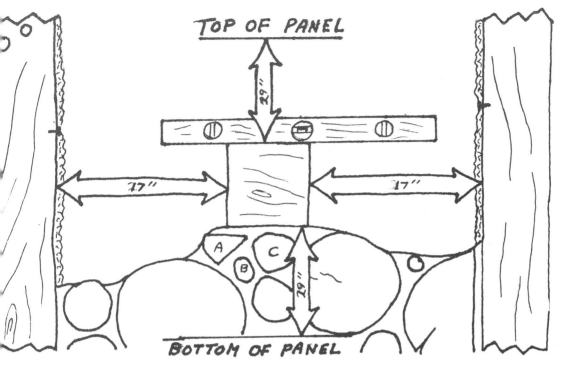

TOP OF PANEL

BOTTOM OF PANEL

5-3. Stained beam-ends add interest to rectangular panels.
They should be centered in the panel and leveled. Centering takes
planning and measuring. Ends A, B, and C were used specifical-
ly to bring the work up to the right height for the beam-end. The
drawing on page 87, Figure 4-20, shows the finished panel.

some of the square panels as focal points.
(See Figure 5-3.)

You might like to take a few log-ends of
the same size and feature them as a design in
some way. The drawings in Figure 5-4 illustrate some possibilities, which—except for the
pentangle—take advantage of the hexagonal
configuration.

To accent the design, use log-ends two
inches longer than usual and allow the whole

HEXAGON   DIAMOND   TRIANGLE

STAR OF DAVID   PENTANGLE
(DIFFICULT)   (VERY DIFFICULT)

5-4. Deliberate designs in a random wall. The shaded ends should be in raised relief and perhaps sanded and varnished. The ends marked x could be bottle-ends.

design to extend an inch proud of the rest of the wall, inside and out. The center log-end could be regular length . . . or it could be a "bottle-end." (See below.)

Design work of this kind takes advance planning—you should put aside special log-ends for the purpose—and it takes time, but it is worth it. Some of the best designs in your house, though, will be those that occur naturally in the random style. We have one panel, for example, where there is the illusion of a flow of small log-ends cascading over a precipice and smashing on a big log-end below.

Another design consideration is the placement of checks. (See Figure 2-4.) Again, we stayed with the random look, but tried to avoid placing checks uppermost in panels where water or snow can collect.

Balance. In general, balance will be achieved if you deplete your various sized log-ends at the same rate. But remember to plan a little for your big pieces or they will accumulate in your pile. Conversely, it's all too easy to use up little log-ends fast. Concentration and self-discipline are necessary to avoid this trap. If you really are short of small pieces (necessary to prevent great expanses of cement), split a clear-grained medium-sized log-end into sixths. The resulting pie-slice shapes are useful and interesting.

Shelves. We have alot of shelves built into our walls, but it would be unreasonable to expect to store cannonballs or pet rocks on log-end shelves. We employed two different types of shelf in our cottage. Figure 5-5 shows individual 16" slat-ends protruding 7" into the room. These make fine display shelves and are grand for candles. Figures 5-5 and 5-6 show a shelf made from one-inch boarding resting on two slat-ends at the same level. *Use a carpenter's level to get this exactly right.* The shelf is placed to give continuity to the adjacent panels.

Coat Pegs and Axe Brackets. Little log-ends sticking out four inches. (See Figure 5-8.)

Stairway. Our stairway to the loft looks as if it were made from log-ends. As a matter of fact, the ash steps do go right through the wall and form stairs both sides, but the whole structure was built before any log-ends were laid in

5-5. (Above) Decorative shelves

5-6. (Below) A one-by-eight shelf ties two walls together.

this panel. The steps are very heavy and the load is completely carried by the three-by-ten runners. Fitting the log-ends around the stairs was exacting work. (We advise laying up the easiest panels first to build up confidence and to improve technique before tackling this kind of panel.) Figure 5-9 shows the work in progress. The two upright log-ends awaiting placement are resting on the inside step of the second ash tread. The third

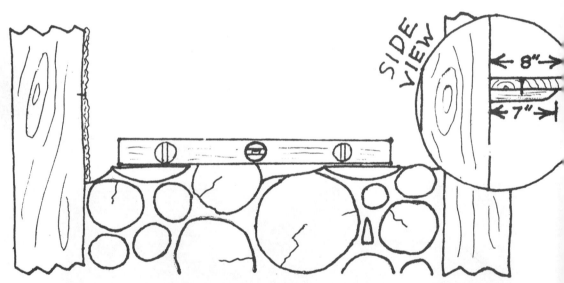

5-7. Shelves, too, take planning. Here, two 16-inch slat-ends are allowed to protrude seven inches into the room. A week later, you can screw a 1"x8" board to the two protrusions, forming, in this case, a 30-inch shelf. Use your level both ways, so that the shelf does not dip toward the room. Check it at the end of the day's work. If the slat ends have dipped a little, use small wooden wedges to bring them back to level. A good piece with which to cap a shelf bracket is another slat-end of regular length. This returns the masonry to a rolling random style.

5-8. Coat pegs and axe brackets.

stairstep is the only one of the six that is made of two separate (18 inch) pieces, because of the interference of the diagonal support members. The other five are a full 45 inches long (18 inches on each side with 9 inches hidden in the wall). Figure 5-10 shows the finished stairs from the inside.

Bottle-Ends. We had seen beer-bottle ma-

5-9. Work in progress on the stairs.

5-10. The finished stairs. The large bottle-end is a terrarium.

sonry in books, but we were concerned about heat loss and the accidental breaking of the necks after the bottles were laid up. So we used a bottle cutter to cut 4½" tumblers from beer and wine bottles and glued the pieces together with an epoxy resin glue. Then we sealed the joint with Mortite, a modeling-clay type substance that is used for all sorts of sealing work. This gave us a kind of double-glazing. It is important that the bottles be dry inside when you seal them. A week after laying up a panel on the south wall, we noticed that there was moisture in one of the bottle-ends. A few weeks later that bottle-end cracked, the only one in the cottage to do so.

The cracked bottle-end, by the way, is hardly noticeable and does not constitute a hazard so we have left it alone. If the situation worsens, I will put on safety goggles and gloves, remove the broken bottle-end with a hammer and chisel, and mortar in a new, properly sealed bottle-end—of a slightly lesser diameter, if necessary.

Another way to make bottle-ends is by gluing two mustard or baby-food jars together. (See Figure 5-11.)

We used thirty-six such bottle-ends in our cottage, mostly as a feature of the panels next to the stairway, which face southeast and southwest. Another panel in the kitchen captures the early morning rays in the summer. (See Figure 5-6.) I wish I could describe the jewellike beauty of the direct rays of the sun playing on a panel of multicolored bottle-ends. (See Figures 5-12 and 5-13.)

We also laid up a gallon storage jar in our wall for use as a terrarium. Loosening or tighten-

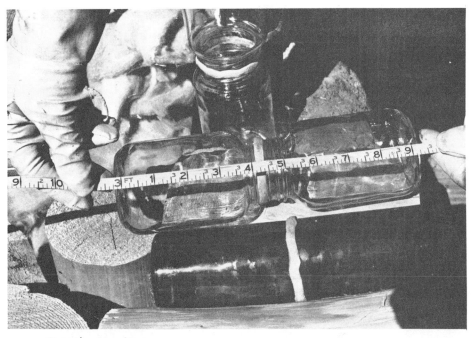

5-11. Bottle-ends...

ing the stained-glass cap regulates the air flow.

    Windows. Although our windows are framed with heavy timbers, stovewood masonry would easily support a window "floating" in a panel. In

5-12.... by day...

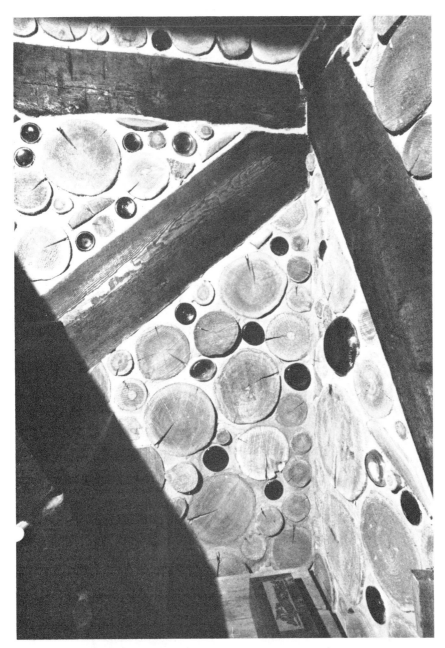

5-13.... and by night.

fact, I have seen pictures of other log-end buildings where this has been done. The following
illustration shows how such a window, framed
with two-by-eights, could be built into a log-end wall.

Old windows like the one shown in Figure 5-14 can often be found at auctions, garage sales, or building demolition sites. We had eight or ten such windows collected from here and there, but we gave them to friends when we realized that our diagonals got in the way of using them in our own cottage.

2"×8"s

5-14

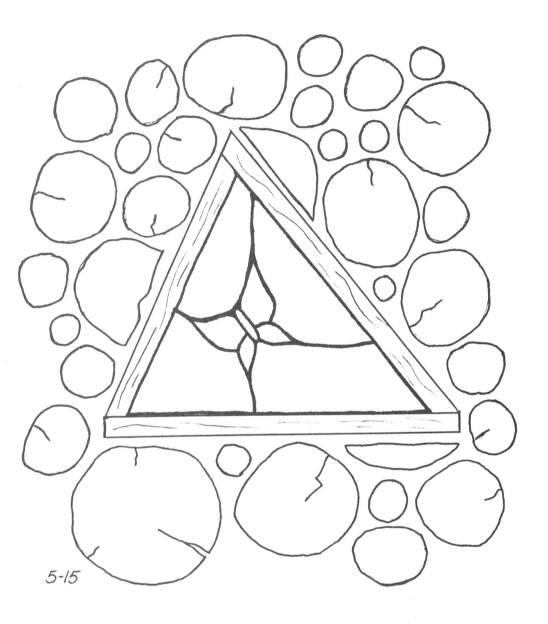

5-15

The floating windows could be of any shape, though curved frames might be difficult unless you are lucky enough to score portholes from a boat being broken up for salvage. I would love to see a log-end house with several randomly spaced portholes as a design feature.

Another possibility: a framed stained-glass panel floating in stovewood masonry. (See Figure 5-15.)

I feel that such a "floating" window should be non-opening, in order to minimize the chance of its loosening in the stovewood masonry by the

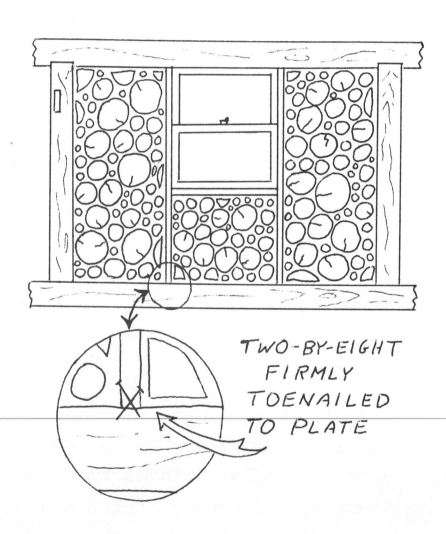

TWO-BY-EIGHT
FIRMLY
TOENAILED
TO PLATE

5-16

vibration of frequent opening and closing. For hinged or sash windows, your surround should be firmly anchored to the framework. (See Figure 5-16.)

The hinged trapezoidal window in Figure 5-6 is framed in similar fashion.

Floating or fixed, leave galvanized roofing nails projecting a quarter inch on the masonry side of all framing to help ensure a good wood-to-mortar bond.

Use Your Imagination. You'll think of all kinds of features to incorporate into your walls. We had to restrain ourselves from using too many outlandish ideas or else we would have had an undesirable hodge-podge look to our cottage. One idea we couldn't resist is shown at the top of the next page.

5-17

5-18. South gable end.

5-19. North gable end.

5-20. West wall showing porch and diagonals.

5-21. The homestead.

5-22. Log-ends, detail.

5-23. Living room.

5-24. Sauna.

FURTHER COMMENTS, PROS AND CONS, COST

6

In an excellent book, *In Harmony With Nature*, by Christian Bruyère (Drake, 1975), stovewood masonry is discussed in two paragraphs on page 42.

"And now we come to the experiment that failed, the eastern position of the south wall. Here we have a cordwood wall made of bone dry cedar rounds which sat in the house for 6 weeks in 100 degree weather. Even though they were aged and dried they still managed to check and crack within their cement frame. I took extreme care every step of the way to make this wall. I even dry mixed the 1-part lime, 2-part Portland cement, 3-part sand mixture before adding water, to keep it from shrinking. But the cement still shrunk. Even with every precaution exercised, before long the cedar rounds were loose in the cement.

"This wall took forever to make. I could only go 18" at a time because so much mortar was needed between each round. Then I had to wait for that portion to dry before going on to the next. The wall is pleasing to look at, but it doesn't have any insulative value because concrete does not hold in heat. When I look at the wall now I say to myself, there is a month's worth of firewood that we could later use."

Well, it's not all a bed of roses, is it? This builder's experience points out the need for vigilance at all times while building with log-ends. I don't think the man is quite right in saying that every precaution was exercised because, in that case, his experiment would have been a success; likely, he was not aware of some of these other precautions.

Log-ends should be air-dried outside. They shouldn't just sit in the house for six weeks, even in 100° weather. Circulation and time are the keys. Dried properly, cedar log-ends should do most, if not all, of their checking *before* they are laid up. Also, the builder's mix was far too strong, almost one to one in terms of masonry cement. Remember, the stronger the mix, the greater the mortar shrinkage.

The pictures which accompany the builder's text show why it took so much time and mortar to lay up his wall. In the whole

6-1. Problems will occur. This particularly nasty check on a big log-end in the south wall has opened a quarter inch since it was laid up. This is about the worst occurence of log-end shrinkage in our cottage. We had to restuff the check.

panel, there are only two small log-ends. There are great diamond and rectangular shapes of mortar between his large log-ends. And I presume the masonry is solid through the wall as there is no mention of a dead-air space or insulation. The builder is right when he says that concrete will not hold in heat, but log-ends are excellent for the purpose, if the time is taken to stuff the checks and insulate the jointing.

If the suggestions in this book are followed, it is possible to lay up an uncomplicated panel measuring five feet by six feet in a day, and the mortar should support all the work without waiting for the lower part to dry. Mortar dries all too fast next to log-ends. Use every trick you can think of to slow down the drying. If the reader, like the builder quoted above, wants to feature stovewood masonry on only one side of the house, why not take an extra precaution and make it the north side, where the sun's rays can't beat down on the wall?

Yes, despite my admitted prejudice in favor of log-ends, it must be admitted that there are pros and cons to their use:

Pros

1. In my (biased) opinion, there is no more beautiful wall than one of stovewood masonry. This method combines the interest of a stone wall with the warmth of wood. And there's no interior decorating!

2. Except for the framework, there is no heavy lifting as in stonework and traditional log cabins. One person can do the work alone, although a helper makes it go a whole lot faster.

3. Cedar is an excellent insulator, but insulate your mortar for a year-round home in northern climes.

4. Cedar resists rot and insects, so your walls should last for a long, long time, especially if you overhang your roof a couple of feet.

5. Trees and deadwood which would be of no use with other types of building might be just fine for stovewood masonry.

6. Stovewood masonry is inexpensive, especially if you consider the saving on insulation. (See below.)

7. It is creative.

8. It is fun.

Cons

1. Stovewood masonry is a lot of exacting, meticulous work.

2. It takes more time, especially in the preparations than most other methods, but less than free-form stone masonry.

3. There is little bond between wood and mortar, so stovewood masonry should not be relied upon as a load-supporting medium, although we have seen this done.

4. Your cedar should be dried at least six months under optimum conditions before laying it up.

5. There's little room for error, as is indicated by the experience recounted at the beginning of this section. Take time to do it right.

Cost

Okay, maybe you've seen references to stovewood masonry before now, and maybe you bought this book because the method appeals to you. Now, if I've done my job, you're perhaps ready to take the plunge and try it yourself. But you've got one more important question. What's all this going to cost?

Rest relieved! Stovewood masonry is a thrifty way to build. Our actual walls, not including the post-and-beam framework, cost:

Log-ends $15, as discussed
                                    in Chapter Two

Saw rental	20
Gasoline	5
Sand	18 (We could have used dark sand free.)
Lime	0 (We were given broken bags at the store where we bought our cement.)
White Portland (3 bags)	20 (Too much.)
Masonry cement (6 bags)	14
Insulation	8
Odds and ends	12 (At most.)
Total	$112

For a 100' perimeter cottage with two log-end gables, a bagatelle. We could have saved on sand and Portland, but we were lucky scoring cedar and lime. The $112, of course, does not reflect the total cost of our cottage. In fact, the masonry walls were easily the most economic part of the structure. But the figure does allow the reader to compare the cost of stovewood masonry with whatever else he might have considered in its stead.

Ten Commandments

1. Use clear cedar, red or white. If no cedar is available, use Douglas fir, western larch, or pine. Avoid white fir, hemlock, spruce, or hardwoods. They will rot.

2. Cut and dry your log-ends as long before they are needed as possible.

3. Plan a house with considerable roof overhang.

4. Build a strong foundation and enclose your stovewood masonry within a sturdy post-and-beam framework.

5. Stuff the checks with insulation just before laying up the log-ends.

6. Dry-mix your mortar before adding water.

7. Do not mix mortar stronger than three to one. Use plenty of lime.

8. Insulate your mortar with fiberglass or sawdust.

9. Hang wet towels on your finished work to prevent the mortar from drying too fast and cracking.

10. Do not build with log-ends if you're in a hurry.

Final Note One: If you've been meticulous in your work and *still* get lots of mortar cracks and small shrinkage gaps next to the log-ends after a few months, mix a pot of thick Thoroseal (a masonry sealer) and apply it liberally to the joints with a half-inch brush. You can get white Thoroseal for about a dollar more than the standard gray. One fifty-pound bag should seal a good-sized log-end house. Even if your walls are perfect, you might consider using Thoroseal for its sealing and coloring properties. In a couple of years, we may decide to apply one or two coats of white Thoroseal to our exterior jointing to seal tiny cracks.

Final Note Two: I will be happy to answer questions personally, but please remember to enclose a stamped self-addressed envelope. Write:

Rob Roy
Log End
R.R. #1, Box 40 C
West Chazy, New York, 12992

And the best o' luck to you!

GLOSSARY

bead of mortar In stovewood masonry, one of
  the two narrow beds of mortar which enclose
  a strip of insulation.

beam-end A short piece of a beam which is
  used in a log-end wall as a design feature,
  the exterior creosoted.

bed In masonry, the mortar upon which a
  brick, stone, or log-end is laid.

checking The natural splitting of a log-end
  (or any piece of wood) by rapid drying.
  Usually, only one "check," or crack, will
  appear on each log-end.

log-end A short (6" to 12") log, preferably
  cedar, one of many mortared together in
  the way that a rank of firewood is stacked.

mortar Generally, a mixture of sand, cement,
  lime, and water, used for bedding and
  pointing bricks, stones, or log-ends. The
  characteristics of mortar depend upon the
  amount of each constituent.

panel A section of stovewood masonry enclosed
  by posts and beams.

pointing The filling of masonry joints with mortar, smoothed with a knife or the point of a trowel. Also "grouting."

proud In masonry, the opposite of recessed. Protrusive.

slat-end A 6" to 12" piece cut from the rough outside slat (or "slab") taken from a log being ripped into lumber.

spud A chisel-like tool for removing bark.

BIBLIOGRAPHY

Airhart, Sharon. "Cord Wood House," *Harrowsmith*, November/December 1976. Pages 54-57.

Bruyére, Christian. *In Harmony With Nature*. New York: Drake, 1975.

Dale, Bruce, and Pat Hutson. "Winter in Snowy Stehekin," *National Geographic*, April, 1974. Page 580.

Hodges, Tom. "The Peeling Spud: A Handy Tool for the Homestead," *The Mother Earth News*, July 1976. Page 122.

Kern, Ken. *The Owner-Built Home*. New York: Charles Scribner's Sons, 1975.

Langsner, Drew and Louise. *Handmade*. New York: Harmony Books, 1974.

Sloane, Eric. *An Age of Barns*. New York: Ballantine, 1974.